ABDO Publishing Company

BUGS!
Ants

Kristin Petrie

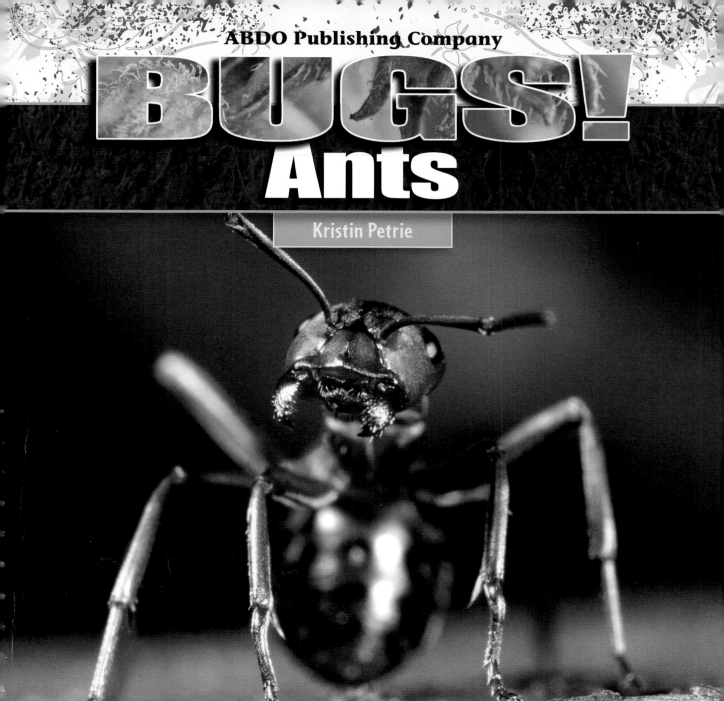

visit us at
www.abdopublishing.com

Published by ABDO Publishing Company, 8000 West 78th Street, Edina, Minnesota 55439.
Copyright © 2009 by Abdo Consulting Group, Inc. International copyrights reserved in all
countries. No part of this book may be reproduced in any form without written permission from the
publisher. The Checkerboard Library™ is a trademark and logo of ABDO Publishing Company.

Printed in the United States.

Cover Photo: Peter Arnold
Interior Photos: Alamy pp. 7, 17; Andy Williams/CritterZone.com p. 22; Getty Images pp. 9, 19, 23;
    iStockphoto pp. 15, 17, 18, 24, 26; Murray S. Blum/Bugwood.org p. 12;
    Paul D. Lemke/CritterZone.com p. 13; Peter Ambruzs/CritterZone.com pp. 14, 20, 27, 29;
    Peter Arnold pp. 1, 5, 17; Photo Researchers pp. 11, 21
Image on page 25 reprinted with permission from *Britannica Elementary Encyclopedia*, © 2006 by
    Encyclopædia Britannica, Inc.

Series Coordinator: BreAnn Rumsch
Editors: Megan M. Gunderson, BreAnn Rumsch
Art Direction & Cover Design: Neil Klinepier

Library of Congress Cataloging-in-Publication Data

Petrie, Kristin, 1970-
  Ants / Kristin Petrie.
     p. cm. -- (Bugs!)
  Includes index.
  ISBN 978-1-60453-062-9
  1. Ants--Juvenile literature. I. Title.

QL568.F7P46 2008
595.79'6--dc22

2008004775

Contents

Abundant Ants

Ants are everywhere! They're in the house, on the driveway, and in the yard. They get into your food, crawl on your skin, and bug your dog. Wherever you go, ants are there.

Like all insects, ants have six legs, three body **segments**, and no bones. Insects make up the largest group of living creatures in the world. And guess what! There are more individual ants than the total number of all other animals combined. No wonder they are everywhere!

Since there are so many ants, we tend to squash them on sight. Sure, it can be gross to see a bunch of ants feasting on your watermelon. But did you ever wonder how they found it? There weren't any ant invaders when you sat down to eat. And now there are hundreds!

While ants can be annoying, they are also pretty impressive. Keep reading to discover some interesting facts about these clever, pesky insects. You may find yourself thinking twice before squashing the next ants you see.

Ants are social creatures. This means they stick together and survive by teamwork. So where you find one ant, you are likely to find many more!

What Are They?

All insects belong to the class Insecta. Within this class, several types of insects belong to the order Hymenoptera. This order includes ants, as well as bees and wasps.

Ants belong to the family Formicidae. The entire family includes around 8,000 species. Some may sound familiar, such as the carpenter ant or the harvester ant. Others are more unusual, such as the leaf-cutter ant or the thief ant.

Each species of ant has a two-word name called a binomial. A binomial combines the genus with a descriptive name, or epithet. For example, a wood ant's binomial is *Formica rufa*.

There sure are a lot of ants! They come in all shapes, sizes, and colors. And, they have varied ways of life. Yet all ant species have something in common. They are social insects that live in organized **colonies**.

BUG BYTES

Ant colonies consist of different types, or castes, of ants. They are queens, males, and workers. Each caste performs a specific job. For example, large workers called soldiers protect the colony.

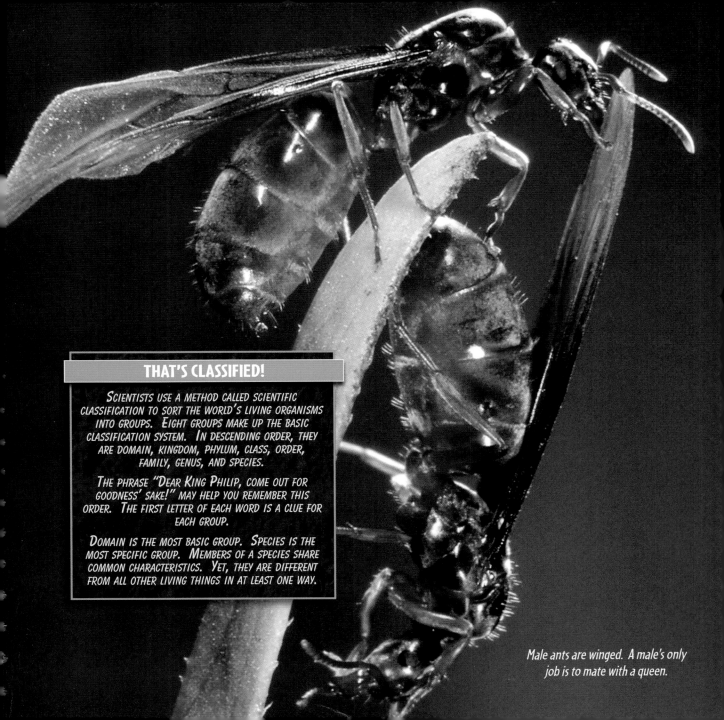

THAT'S CLASSIFIED!

Scientists use a method called scientific classification to sort the world's living organisms into groups. Eight groups make up the basic classification system. In descending order, they are domain, kingdom, phylum, class, order, family, genus, and species.

The phrase "Dear King Philip, come out for goodness' sake!" may help you remember this order. The first letter of each word is a clue for each group.

Domain is the most basic group. Species is the most specific group. Members of a species share common characteristics. Yet, they are different from all other living things in at least one way.

Male ants are winged. A male's only job is to mate with a queen.

Body Parts

Did you squash a few ants to save your watermelon? If so, you may have noticed a crunch. The crunching sound came from each ant's exoskeleton. An exoskeleton is a stiff outer covering that is much like a shell. Ants don't have bones, so the hard exoskeleton protects their **organs**.

The exoskeleton is divided into three body **segments**. These are the head, the thorax, and the abdomen. An ant's head features some important parts. To reach the head, you must get past the sharp mandibles. Mandibles stick out near the ant's mouth like two sharp blades. Their functions include carrying items, cutting, and fighting.

Behind the mandibles are the maxillae, or jaws. These are for chewing food into tiny pieces. A chunk of watermelon would never fit into an ant's tiny mouth. Therefore, its jaws work hard to break down food. Then, the food is moved from the ant's maxillae into its mouth.

Ant mandibles come in many shapes and sizes. Predatory ants have long, sharp mandibles. Common household ant mandibles are much smaller.

Feelers, or antennae, are an important part of an ant's head. These are used for communication, smell, touch, and taste. Ants communicate with each other by releasing **pheromones**. These chemicals have different smells, depending on the message.

Ants use their sense of smell to identify objects around them. These include predators and other ants. One ant used her antennae to sniff her way to your watermelon. When she got there, she sent a message to her friends. The message told them where food was. They used their antennae to smell the pheromones she sent and to identify the meaning of her message.

Antennae also allow ants to feel vibrations. These sensations provide important information. This could be the location of danger or the way home. In addition, tiny sensory hairs cover most ant bodies and antennae. These hairs allow them to feel, much like the hairs on your arms.

Ants use their eyes to sense the world around them, too. An ant's eyes are much like a fly's eyes. They are bulging compound eyes. Compound eyes have many lenses connected as one. This allows ants to easily see movement.

An ant is able to identify other ants by
rubbing antennae with them.

Next to an ant's head is its thorax. This middle **segment** contains most of the ant's muscles. These tiny but powerful muscles control six legs. Each jointed leg ends in a sharp claw. These claws allow an ant to climb and walk upside down. If an ant has wings, they are also controlled by muscles in the thorax.

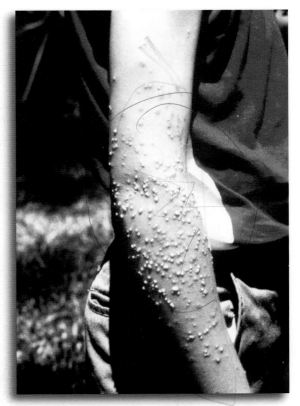

The rear end of an ant's body is called the abdomen. Two sections make up the abdomen. The first section is called the petiole. This rounded nub is the smallest section of an ant's body. In fact, it looks like the ant's waist. Some ants have one petiole and others have two.

The second part of the abdomen is called the gaster. It looks like a large bulb and contains two

Fire ants are known for their painful sting. These ants grab on to victims with their mouthparts. Then, they inject their poison with a stinger. Within hours of being stung, victims experience swelling, redness, and pus-filled bumps.

stomachs. The first stomach is called the crop. It is for food storage. Food can be **regurgitated** from this stomach to feed other ants. The second stomach is for **digestion**.

The abdomen of some ant species also contains a poisonous sac. This sac is used as a defense against enemies. Some ants **inject** their poison through a stinger at the end of the abdomen. Other ants spray their poison. Either way, enemies should beware!

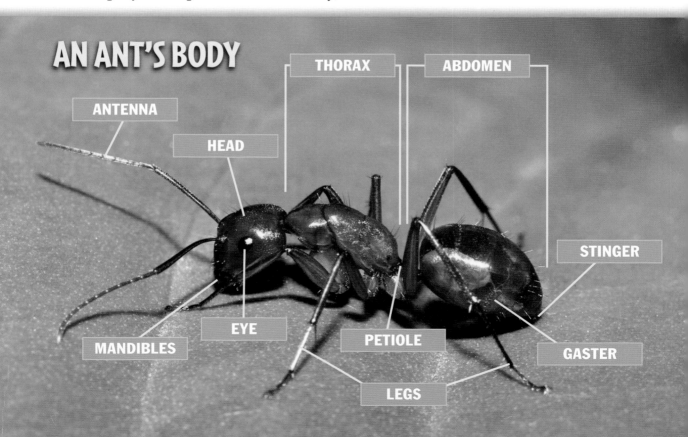

AN ANT'S BODY

THORAX

ABDOMEN

ANTENNA

HEAD

STINGER

EYE

MANDIBLES

PETIOLE

GASTER

LEGS

The Inside Story

Ants need to breathe oxygen and drink water, just like you.

Inside an ant, several systems and **organs** work hard to keep its tiny body moving. An ant's respiratory system is much different from a human's! This is because ants do not have lungs. Instead, oxygen enters an ant's body through spiracles. These are tiny holes in the exoskeleton.

An ant's circulatory system is called an open system. This means the ant's blood flows freely inside its body, rather than through veins. Ant blood is called hemolymph. The ant's heart is a long tube. It keeps the hemolymph moving from end to end.

One long **nerve** makes up an ant's nervous system. This nerve runs from the ant's head to its rear end. It delivers signals from the ant's brain to its legs, antennae, and other body parts. This helps the ant move its body.

BUG BYTES

The odorous house ant gets its name from the smell it produces. When squashed, these tiny ants stink like rotten coconuts!

Ants rely on their body systems to help them navigate the giant objects in their world.

Transformation

An ant's life cycle begins when a queen ant mates with a male ant. Males and queens have wings, so mating takes place in flight. After mating, the male dies and the queen sheds her wings.

Then, the queen prepares a new home. There, she lays thousands of **fertilized** eggs. As a first-time mom, the queen must care for her eggs alone. Once the first generation of babies has grown, they become workers. The workers care for each new generation of eggs.

After several days, the eggs hatch into larvae. Larvae are white, wormlike creatures. They stay very busy eating. Worker ants bring them food nonstop. The larvae eat just about anything. The selections include other larvae, insects, and partially **digested** foods.

When the larvae are nice and stuffed, they each weave a cocoon around themselves. Now they are called pupae. Inside their cocoons, the pupae make an amazing transformation. They come out as fully grown adult ants. These ants may be workers, soldiers, or males. The progression of these stages in an ant's life is called complete **metamorphosis**.

LIFE CYCLE OF AN ANT

EGG

ADULT

LARVA

PUPA

Ant Appetites

Now we know that ant larvae eat some interesting types of food. As for adult ants, we've always known they like our food! They'll dig into whatever is on your plate.

In their own **habitats**, ants eat a wide variety of foods. These include plants and animals. Favorite foods are honeydew and small insects. Do you know the most chilling part of the ant diet? It is other ants!

Despite the wide variety in an ant's diet, these creatures can **digest** only liquid foods. After stealing your cookie, the ant chews it to a paste. Inside its mouth, liquid is squeezed from the paste and swallowed. The ant spits out the dry leftovers.

Predatory ants can be forceful with their prey. Their sharp mandibles help them attack their meals.

Leaf-cutter ants can strip a tree of its leaves in just a few hours. The ants take the leaves into their nest. There, ants chew on the leaves until they break down into a wet pulp. A fungus grows on the pulp, which feeds the entire colony.

Aphids are sometimes called ant cows. This is because some ant species milk these bugs for honeydew. Then, the ants share the honeydew with one another.

The liquid food travels to one of the ant's stomachs. Most likely, it will enter the crop. This is the pouch that holds food for sharing. That's right! After working so hard for a drop of food, an ant will spit it out for another ant.

When an ant is hungry, it moves liquid food from its crop to its second stomach. There, food is **digested** and absorbed for growth. Waste products then leave the ant's body from its anus.

A SWEET TREAT

Honeydew is a mixture of sugar and water. Worker ants acquire honeydew from other small insects, such as aphids. Workers bring this sweet mixture back to their nest. If it is not eaten immediately, some species store the honeydew in an unusual place.

The abdomens of some worker ants, called repletes, serve as storage. These unfortunate workers are known as honey pot ants. They are so full of honeydew that they look like a pot of honey! In fact, honey pot ants become so bloated that they cannot walk. So, hungry ants visit their bloated coworkers when they want a tasty snack.

Life in a Colony

Living underground provides protection from all kinds of weather conditions. When temperatures are extremely hot or cold, ants tunnel to the deepest levels of their homes.

Where do ants live? You might see them in your kitchen or at a picnic. It may seem that ants live everywhere you look. In fact, ants do live in most areas of the world.

However, ants prefer warm places to cold ones. So you will probably not find a single ant in Antarctica. On the other hand, rain forests are jam-packed with ants. They can even be found in the hottest deserts, where food sources are scarce.

How do ants do it? They are tough creatures. Ants are excellent at adapting to their surroundings. In the scorching desert, they tunnel deep into the cool ground. Where meals are scarce, they search nonstop to find food and water.

ANTS ON THE MOVE

Army ants do not make a home anywhere. Instead, they carry everything with them. This includes food, larvae, and other ants. These ants get their name from the way they behave. They march in wide lines like an army, devouring everything in their path.

While on the move, these carnivores will attack larger insects, animals, and even human beings! It's no wonder many people leave their homes when these ant swarms approach!

One tropical ant species lives up in the trees. Known as weaver ants, the colony's larvae produce silk. This material is used to bind leaves together to make a nest.

Wherever its location in the world, an ant **colony** must make a home. Ant homes have different names. The most common are anthills, ant mounds, and ant nests.

Anthills and ant mounds get their names from the dirt that surrounds their front doors. A pile of dirt forms when ants tunnel underground. Ants dig down into the earth and remove dirt to make hallways and rooms. The larger the anthill, the larger the underground home.

Underground ant homes can be very **complex**. Many chambers make up their homes, somewhat like yours. For example, one chamber may be the kitchen, or food area. Other chambers are bedrooms, or resting rooms. Last are the nurseries, where all those eggs and larvae are kept.

An anthill is like an underground city. Some anthills extend down into the ground more than 30 feet (9 m)!

Other ant species live in trees or on leaves. Perhaps you have seen the holes ants make in fallen trees. These ants tunnel into dry wood and live inside the trunk. This helps recycle the dead tree's **nutrients** for growing plants to use.

Beware!

In addition to ants, anteaters snack on termites, larvae, worms, and some fruits.

Ants must watch out for many predators. Spiders, snakes, and birds eat ants as a main part of their diet. And then there is the most obvious predator of all. Can you guess which animal it is? It's the anteater, of course!

The anteater has a snout shaped like a tube. It also has a long, sticky tongue. The anteater dives right into an ant's underground home with its long, curved claws. Then, the anteater pokes its tongue deep into the ant's nest for a tasty meal.

What else do ants need to be wary of? In addition to larger enemies, they have to watch out for other ants. Other enemies include you! Most humans think ants are pests. We step on many at a time and destroy their homes.

Ants stand a much better chance against creatures their own size. Many ants attack their enemies in a massive swarm. They use their sharp mandibles to bite. Others use their poisonous stinger to protect themselves.

Social organization helps ants attack larger creatures.

Ants and You

With so many ants around, it can be hard not to find them annoying. They always seem to find your snacks. In addition, some ants bite or sting. Despite these negatives, ants play an important role in nature.

Ants are great cleaners. They haul away bug carcasses and consume dead plants and other debris. They also break down fallen leaves and wood. Do ants just like a tidy place? This is possible. However, it is more likely that ants use the debris in their homes or for food.

Some people really like ants. For instance, farmers appreciate ants for eating bugs that kill crops. Gardeners welcome ants for the same reason. And, everyone should thank ants for tunneling in the ground. This brings oxygen into the soil, keeping it healthy. Healthy soil means crops and other plants will grow successfully.

Now you know that ants can be useful. So, you may want to leave them alone if they are not bothering you. Instead of stomping

BUG BYTES

Pharaoh ants are gross pests that love hospitals. There, they feast on sealed packages of supplies. They also enjoy used bloody bandages and even surgical wounds!

Ants are incredibly strong. With their jaws, ants can lift and carry 20 to 50 times their own weight. If a 200-pound (91-kg) man were as strong, he could lift 3 tons (2.7 t) with his teeth!

on the next ant you see, you should watch it! Look for its interesting body parts. Watch it use its cool antennae. See how it interacts with its friends. You just might start to appreciate ants on your watermelon!

Glossary

colony - a population of plants or animals in a certain place that belongs to a single species.

complex - having many parts, details, ideas, or functions.

digest - to break down food into substances small enough for the body to absorb. The process of digesting food is called digestion.

fertilize - to make fertile. Something that is fertile is capable of growing or developing.

habitat - a place where a living thing is naturally found.

inject - to forcefully introduce a substance into something.

metamorphosis - the process of change in the form and habits of some animals during development from an immature stage to an adult stage.

nerve - one of the stringy bands of nervous tissue that carries signals from the brain to other organs.

nutrient - a substance found in food and used in the body to promote growth, maintenance, and repair.

organ - a part of an animal or a plant that is composed of several kinds of tissues and that performs a specific function. The heart, liver, gallbladder, and intestines are organs of an animal.

pheromone - a chemical substance produced by an animal. It serves as a signal to other individuals of the same species to engage in some kind of behavior.

regurgitate - to throw back out again, especially partially digested food.

segment - any of the parts into which a thing is divided or naturally separates.

How Do You Say That?

antennae - an-TEH-nee
Formicidae - fawr-MIHS-uh-dee
hemolymph - HEE-muh-lihmf
Hymenoptera - heye-muh-NAHP-truh
larvae - LAHR-vee
maxillae - mak-SIH-lee
metamorphosis - meh-tuh-MAWR-fuh-suhs
petiole - PEH-tee-ohl
pheromone - FEHR-uh-mohn
pupae - PYOO-pee
regurgitate - ree-GUHR-juh-tayt

Web Sites

To learn more about ants, visit ABDO Publishing Company on the World Wide Web at **www.abdopublishing.com**. Web sites about ants are featured on our Book Links page. These links are routinely monitored and updated to provide the most current information available.

Index